EQUIP YOUR CHILD FOR LIFE

Seven Tools Your Children
Should Not Leave Home Without

TONY PETERS

Published by

T P PUBLICATIONS
4 Pegamoid Road.
Edmonton. London.
N18 2NG

ISBN 978-1-874332-66-4

Copyright © 2014 by Tony Peters

TABLE OF CONTENT

PREFACE

Raising children is such an important responsibility for parents; and it's a shame that we are not doing more as a society to help parents get it right.

We put a lot more effort into preparing people to drive cars, cook food, cut hair or plumb our kitchen sink, than we put into helping parents raise the next generation of leaders, ministers, politicians and law-makers. Both our education and health-care systems are guilty of this.

The result is that our society is at a crossroad and our children are leaving home without the tools they need to make it in a complicated and often confusing world.

Parents almost always want to leave a legacy for their children. Unfortunately, many parents think of legacy only in the form of tangible things like money, houses, education or possessions.

However, lasting legacy is much bigger than stuff. It is about integrity, humility, generosity, fairness, and faith – intangible virtues that make our children positive contributing members of society.

It is my goal in this concise book to parents, to contribute my thoughts to the ongoing debate, and to share some well-worn tools that parents of all ages have deposited in their children before sending them out into this capricious world to fend for themselves.

INTRODUCTION

Train up a child in the way he should go, and when he is old he will not depart from it. (Proverbs 22:6.)

Preparing children for an effective life in society is our responsibility as parents. But, we can't do our job well, if we don't accept this responsibility joyfully and wholeheartedly, and face it confidently and seriously.

If as parents, we can't see why our children's developmental needs should supersede our social life or career progress, the chances that we would make wholesome decisions about how we raise them are likely to be very slim.

We may, for instance, think it's okay to abandon little Johnny to numerous child-minders and strangers during his formative years. Or we may decide to ship our vulnerable Vicky off to boarding school (a thousand mile from home) without thinking about the damage it will do to her identity or sense of wellbeing.

The Law of Consequences

The dire consequences of decisions like this are all around us. We wonder why our children are so angry and aggressive by the time they start Kindergarten. We wonder why our sons are ending up in gangs and prison. We wonder why many of our daughters are running off with men twice their age; and we wonder why they are getting themselves pregnant instead of completing their education.

Well, we don't need to wonder why any more. We just need to know that we live in a world that is governed by 'cause and effect'. Some people call it the Principle of Causation and others call it the Law of Consequences.

Irrespective of what we call it, the point is that we reap what we sow, and we harvest what we plant. That's why it is important to take a long, hard look at how we are raising our children, and make the investments necessary to grow the kind of children we will all be proud of for decades to come.

Responsibility 101

There is a very sad story in the Bible that was put there to show us how important it is for parents to take the responsibility of raising their children seriously.

Eli was Israel's High Priest. He was a Levite called by God to minister before Him. Eli was the only one allowed into the very presence of God (the Holy of Holies) once a year. He took the people's sins to God & brought back God's promises, mercies and blessings to them.

But Eli had two sons who were corrupt and immoral. They took delight in bullying and terrorising the people who came to sacrifice to God. Eli's two sons hired bullies to 'rob' the people of their sacrifice before it was properly offered to God.

Although Eli was the most powerful man in the Country, this blatant and ungodly behaviour by his sons was taking place right under his nose. Eli was, to all intent and purpose, an absentee dad. He did not restrain them. He failed to discipline them. And, worst of all, he allowed them to carry on serving as priests – when he should have relieved them of their jobs.

Notice what God said about Eli:

> ***Then the LORD said to Samuel: "Behold, I will do something in Israel at which both ears of everyone who hears it will tingle. "In that day I will perform against Eli all that I have spoken concerning his house, from beginning to end. "For I have told him that I will judge his house forever for the iniquity which he knows, because his sons made themselves vile, and he did not restrain them. "And therefore I have sworn to the house of Eli that the iniquity of Eli's house shall not be atoned for by sacrifice or offering forever."***
>
> (1 Samuel 3:11-14.)

The family knew what was right, but nobody chose to do the right thing. That's why in the passage above, God decided to judge the whole family. And, He raised up Samuel to replace them.

The question is Why? Why did Eli have to suffer for his children's behaviour? He was punished because he did not exercise the basic responsibility of a good parent.

Another reason is that God wants us (the readers) to know how grievous it is to bring children into the world and not give them the tools they need to live right, to love God and to be up-standing citizens who represent God well in society.

Apprentices and Toolboxes

When I was growing up, there was a carpenter who lived behind our house. He had an apprentice with him for about 3 years. During that season, the master carpenter taught his apprentice a variety of skills and got him to make a variety of furniture to practice what he had learnt.

At the end of the apprenticeship, the young man got his 'freedom' and was given his own new set of tools in a specially engraved toolbox. I still remember him proudly admiring his spanking new toolbox. That apprentice also received a certificate saying he had learnt the trade successfully and was ready to set-up his carpentry workshop.

Tools for Life

I share this memory because I am convinced that God wants us to see and treat our children like little apprentices too. Our children too need certain skills or tools for life. They need tools that would make them successful as they deal with the stresses of life.

They need tools to help them excel in their relationships, in decision-making, in their finances, in their roles in society and in their responsibilities as parents one day.

They need the tools:

- To help them stay faithful and committed to God.
- To maintain and grow wholesome relationships.
- To manage their finances and investments well.
- To choose the right vocation or career path.
- To find and collaborate successfully with a spouse.
- To excel in the market place of competing ideas.
- To help them live a balanced and healthy life.
- To navigate the complex maze of choices.
- To help them develop a life of integrity.

- To manage their home and raise the next generation of children.

No Perfect Parents

Raising children is never easy, and there are no perfect parents; but if you would diligently do your part, God will do the part you can't do. All He asks is for us to train up our children in the way that they should go. If we do, He promises that our children will become the godly men and women that they were birthed to be.

I am not a child psychologist or sociologist, but for over 13 years in a public school I taught hundreds of children between the ages of 11 and 18. My wife and I have also raised our two children.

So in the rest of this book, I would like to suggest 7 tools that I believe we must endeavour to place in our children's toolbox for life. By the grace of God, my wife and I are seeing them work in our grown-up children, and we are confident that they will work for yours too.

CHAPTER 1

Our Children Need A Solid Foundation For Faith

Faith is the confidence that what we hope for will actually happen... (Hebrews 11:1.)

Our children come into the world with no faith, no beliefs and no opinions. So it's our duty as parents to give them a strong foundation for faith in the living God. I believe there are a number of very good reasons to do so.

- **Firstly,** they are your children, and I'm sure that you want them to have the strong convictions that you have come to trust. No saved, redeemed, born again and fully devoted Christian ever wants less for their children.

- **Secondly,** your children's faith in God and their commitment to His ways will determine their behaviour, their attitude to life, their passions, their core choices, and their world-views.

- **Thirdly,** their faith will in the final analysis determine their eternal destiny. It would determine where they spend eternity. Whether it would be in the presence of their Creator or in the eternal anguish of their adversary.

So if you really love your children, you will take this foremost of responsibilities very seriously. Failure to do so means that your children are going to have to source their spiritual foundations from books, or from the media, or from lecturers and gurus who may not have their best interest at heart.

Consider God's stark commandments to his people soon after they were freed from slavery:

> ***"You shall love the LORD your God with all your heart, with all your soul, and with all your strength. "And these words which I command you today shall be in your heart. "You shall teach them diligently to your children, and shall talk of them when you sit in your house, when you walk by the way, when you lie down, and when you rise up. "You shall bind them as a sign on your hand, and they shall be as frontlets between your eyes. "You shall write them on the doorposts of your house and on your gates.*** (Deuteronomy 6:5-9.)

Notice that God commands parents to:

- First of all, love God completely themselves.
- Then, teach their children to do the same.
- Talk to them about faith at every opportunity.
- Use signs, banners, pictures, ornaments, songs, (and whatever else is available) to communicate the essence of their faith to their children.

In other words, God wanted those ancient Hebrew parents to be proactive and intentional about raising their children with an awareness of (and love for) God.

Take the Initiative

Many years ago, I remember asking a parent of one of my students why her son didn't go to Church with her. Her reply shocked me. She said she didn't want to influence him with her beliefs; and was waiting for him to decide what path to take, when he was old enough to make that decision.

I wanted to laugh out loud, but I restrained myself. What this mother failed to realise was that (whether she liked it or not) her son was already being heavily influenced by popular opinion, by celebs, by television programs, by classmates, by the internet, by atheist and by books designed to introduce them to homo-sexual practices, witchcraft, and the occult.

God wants you to take the initiative, when it comes to the faith of your children, before the world gets them confused. That is why He gave them to you. You are your children's earthly guide until they leave home. You should want them to follow your example, if you believe you have the truth. That's really what parenting is about!

God wants you to give your children every possible advantage to get to know Him and believe in Him, before Satan gets the chance to steal their heart. So be the first to give your children a million reasons to believe in God. It would save you a lot of heartache in the future.

Your Kids Need To See God Through You

'How do I get my Children to know and love God?' you may ask.

You do it:

- By the way you praise and worship God.

- By the way you sincerely talk to Him in front of them.

- By the way you respect God and do what He commands.

- By how you trust Him in the midst of challenges and trials.

- By how you include Him and talk about Him in your discussions.

This is so important because your children can't see God until they see Him through you. They start to catch a glimpse of who God is through your behaviour, your attitude, your actions and your speech.

If you are kind, forgiving and loving, God becomes kind, forgiving and loving to them. If you are critical and judgmental, God's image in their little mind is tainted and marred. I don't know why it seems to work that way, but I have seen enough examples to convince me that parents often set the template for their children's initial view of God, by how they behave.

Your children will learn to read you before they learn to read the Bible. Whatever you do or say in front of them will leave an indelible mark on their tiny souls. So pray for the grace to live a life before them that constantly points them to the reality of God's existence and nature.

The world we live in is programmed to give our children a reason to doubt the existence of a good God. Billboards are springing up to persuade them that God is dead. Books are being written to convince them that God is not good. And, lectures are being promoted on the internet to lure our children away from their Creator.

If we don't proactively engage our children in a vibrant, Bible-based faith life (while they are young), there are plenty of harmful and contagious ideas out there to sway them away from the faith, as they get older.

Rewards of a Solid Foundation for Faith

Children with a solid foundation for faith, invariably become very God-conscious. They become sensitive to His voice and His presence; and I would say that 90% of the time, they would eventually turn their lives over to Him.

As the Bible affirms: If we properly train and equip our children in line with their God-given purposes, they will stay on that path indefinitely. No matter what happens when they are young, they will not stray from the path when they are older. That's what Proverbs 22 and verse 6 promises us.

A solid foundation of faith will:

- Help your children develop a God-consciousness.
- Help them to value their life and the lives of others.
- Help them to develop a more positive attitude to life.
- Help them make sound decisions and choices.
- Give them a strong moral compass for life.
- Help them develop a balanced perspective of life.
- Help them deal better with life's challenges and losses.
- Give them hope when situations look hopeless or bleak.

How to Help Your Children Develop a Solid Foundation for Faith

1. Get serious with God yourself: You can't fool a child when it comes to walking with God because they are always watching you. They may hear what you say, but they'll tend to do what you do. So if you are not serious with God, they will copy you. Get serious with God, because it's never too late to start.

2. Become the person you want your child to be: Children have a knack for copying the attitudes and habits of the core adults in their life. So if you want your children to be generous, be generous yourself. If you want them to be kind and caring, be kind and caring yourself. Be the person you want your kids to be, because they will get their moral bearings from you.

3. Insist on living an authentic life before your children: There is nothing that annoys young people more than hypocrisy. Parents often wonder why their teenage children are rebellious. Eight out of ten times, I am convinced that the reason has to do with a lack of integrity on the part of the parents. When children see this, their world is turned upside down – and rebellion takes over.

Unfortunately, Eli failed to live this way in front of his children and suffered the consequences. Read the rest of the story and you'll discover that Eli lost everything. He lost his position, his children and his life. What a sad ending to the story of a man who held the highest spiritual office in the land.

Whatever else you do, give your children a foundation for faith from the moment they can observe and understand what you are doing. Pray in front of them; read the Bible in front of them; give in front of them; help others in front of them; and worship God in front of them.

If you do, they will know that God is important, and they will seek Him in their lives too. The chance of this ever happening on its own is low, if you fail in your responsibility to your children. So don't fail! Make it your life's goal to leave your children with a solid foundation for faith in God.

> ***Train up a child in the way he should go, And when he is old he will not depart from it.***
> (Proverbs 22:6.)

CHAPTER 2

Our Children Need A Sense Of Purpose

You can make many plans, but the Lord's purpose will prevail... (Proverbs 19:21.)

Don't let your children leave home without helping them to understand what God put them on this earth for. Don't assume that your children know why they are here. Quiz them about it. Call a family meeting if need be, but get your children talking about their reason for being alive on planet earth.

Our children may think their purpose on earth is to become a footballer, a singer, a dancer, solicitor, an engineer or athlete, or even a bus driver. But as parents, one of our jobs is to help them see the bigger picture. There is nothing wrong with a career or a dream job, but that is not enough to satisfy the human soul.

We are to help our children develop a sense of purpose that is bigger than their pet attractions, their future fantasies, or even their dream careers. We must help them define what is important in life and help them do everything they can to accomplish it.

Give them a Bigger Vision

For instance, in our household over 15 years ago, my wife and I sat down with our children before they hit their teenage years and spelt out (in language they could understand) what our purpose as a family was going to be for the foreseeable future.

Since I was being led to plant a new Church in our Community, we agreed that our united family purpose was to worship and serve our God faithfully, and to the best of our abilities, help people to serve and worship Him too. I tried to help them to see how pleased God would be with our family and how much He would bless us individually and as a family, if we did what He was asking us to do.

I remember trying to paint a picture of the value of transformed lives to them. At that time, we didn't know who else would be joining us to start this new Church-plant, so I shared with my children how I would love them to help their mum and I with this new Church plant.

My son, who was 12 at the time, agreed to help with the music if I bought a keyboard that he could learn to play. My daughter, who was 9, agreed to help with the children who come to visit. And, my wife agreed to do anything that needed doing.

That one discussion was all it took to place an enduring sense of purpose in my children. I am still blown away to see how they were animated to serve the Church joyfully and to give of their time, talents and treasures sacrificially.

Today, when I look at the impact our children have made in our Church, I am so grateful that God led my wife and I to give them a bigger sense of purpose when they were still fairly young.

The history of our Church cannot be written without an impressive list of the contributions our children have made to get the Church to where it is today. All because our children caught hold of an enduring sense of purpose at an early age!

Give them something to Live for

You too will have to find something that can give your children a reason to love life and serve people. If not, they may choose a corrupt or ignoble purpose, or even despair of life itself.

Why? Because life abhors a vacuum!

When young people don't have a burning sense of purpose, they get fidgety and restless, and the devil finds work for them. All you need to do is to look at the number of young people committing suicide in our society; or the number of young people in juvenile detention, to realise how devastating a lack of purpose can be for young people.

What to teach them

- Teach your children that they are here to glorify God with their lives.

- Teach them that their Creator put them here to help make a difference.

- Take them to charity events or food kitchens that need help and show them how to help.

- Challenge them to make their lives count on earth – to be kind, compassionate, generous, respectful, humble, creative and fair to all.

- Expose them to ordinary people who have done extraordinary things, to humble people who served humanity, and to people who are still making an impact in the world.

- Show them how to give. Show them how to serve. Teach them how to sacrifice certain things for people who don't have as much as they do. Teach them not just to think of themselves, but to think more of others too.

That's what it is going to take to help your children develop a strong sense of purpose.

Children with a strong sense of purpose:

- Are happier and more fulfilled.
- Are more focused and responsible.
- Are less distracted and more productive.
- Avoid time wasters and dream killers.
- Behave better and achieve more... because they're doing what they are gifted to do and love it.

Helping your children to develop their own sense of purpose is never easy. They may even think that you are trying to control their lives. All you can do is continue to assure them that you have their best interest at heart – and as they get older they will come to appreciate your reasons for taking them on this journey.

Remind them often that you only want what is best for them and what God wants for them. Stay prayerful through the process, so that God can show you what to do and what not to do. Keep praying to hear His voice deep down in your heart, guiding your decisions and your discussions with your children.

Keep reading books, attending workshops or listening to other experienced parents whose wisdom might come in handy. God will see your heart and your desire to give your children the best upbringing possible, and He will help you.

***Come boldly to the throne of our gracious God.
There we will receive his mercy, and we will find
grace to help us when we need it most.***
(Hebrews 4:16.)

Don't let your children leave home without a clear and godly sense of purpose. It will help them to be more focused and productive through the ups and downs of life. It will also make help them choose a more intentional and responsible path.

**When you discover your purpose, it will raise
you out of any situation that tries to keep
you from fulfilling it.**

CHAPTER 3

Our Children Need A Sense Of Gratitude

Oh, give thanks to the Lord, for He is good! And His mercy endures forever.
(Psalm 136:1.)

Let gratitude be the pillow upon which you kneel to say your nightly prayer.
— Maya Angelou

These days many of our children are growing up with an 'entitlement mentality'. That is because everything gets given to them by parents who are trying to compensate for their regular absence or their minimal parenting.

Kids who are hardly out of Kindergarten want iPhones, iPads, Galaxies, X-boxes and a host of other gadgets and luxury items that cost an arm and a leg. But giving our children all the expensive stuff they want is not only fuelling an 'entitlement mentality', but it demotivates them.

Realising this, we taught our children to contribute something to whatever they wanted that was not a necessity. We figured out that if they saved for something they wanted, they would want fewer things, and are more likely to appreciate them when they get them.

It worked! Our children not only picked up the illusive habit of saving, but learnt to 'cut their coat according to the cloth they had'. They picked up so many other life skills and virtues that frankly set them on a path to living successfully.

For instance:

- They learnt to appreciate money.
- They learnt not to be wasteful.
- They learnt to be self-sufficient.
- They learnt to be prudent and frugal.
- They learnt to stretch their resources.
- They learnt to be creative and industrious.
- They learnt not to throw away perfectly usable things.
- They learnt to wait patiently till they could afford the things they wanted.
- They learnt to stay out of debt when many of their mates were falling helplessly into the credit trap.

Today, I am so proud of my children's saving and spending habits. I've watched them save thousands of pounds from the day they started working till today. I've listened to them debate whether a certain gadget was a **need** or a **want** – whether it was a **necessity** or a **luxury**. And, I've had the pleasure of hearing them say, "Dad, we haven't forgotten what you taught us!"

Teach your children to be grateful for what they have, on the way to what they want. Teach them to count their blessings – to focus on the good things they have and to express their gratitude daily for those things.

Teach them to be thankful for the rain, the sunshine, the birds, the moon, the air they breathe, the food they eat, the trees that rustle in the garden, the water that flows from the bathtub, and the bed on which they sleep.

Teach them that gratitude is a magnetic attitude. It opens the door for more to come into their lives. It attracts favour, blessings and abundance.

Teach them that gratitude stops grumbling and complaining. You can't be grateful and ungrateful at the same time. You can't appreciate your blessings and complain in the same breath.

Teach them that the things they are grateful for tend to stick around and increase. If they appreciate their friends, those friends will tend to stick around. If they show their gratitude to their teachers, those teachers will tend to like them too.

Let your children know that:

- Gratitude is a magnetic attitude.
- It's a virtue that sees the invisible.
- It changes our feelings and expectations.
- It dispels depression and attracts abundance.
- It turns the little we have into more than enough.

Alphonse Karr once said, **"Some people grumble that roses have thorns; I am grateful that thorns have roses."** What a powerful lesson.

Alphonse had learnt to look for the diamond in the rough. That's what an attitude of gratitude will do for you and your children.

The Old Testament Jews murmured and complained all through their extraordinary journey in the wilderness, because they lacked this sense of gratitude. They displeased God in the same way as we displease Him today when we complain and murmur in the midst of blessings.

The good old hymn says it best:

> Count your blessings, name them one by one
> Count your blessings, see what God has done
> Count your blessings, name them one by one
> And it will surprise you, what the Lord has done.

"God gave you a gift of 86,400 seconds today. Have you used one to say thank you?"
— William Arthur Ward

How do you teach your children to be grateful?

- By being truly thankful and grateful yourself.

- By demonstrating gratitude for everything – in front of them.

- By insisting that they be thankful for whatever they get.

- By helping them to see how blessed and fortunate they are.

- By exposing them to the poverty and lack that is all around them.

- By encouraging them to give something back to Society, to their teachers, to their Church, and to their Creator.

- By helping them to appreciate the intangible miracles of life – like the air they breath, the beauty of the Sunset, or the privilege of having eyes to see it all.

When children don't learn to be grateful or thankful for what they have:

- They become **envious** of what other people have – and soon get overcome by greed.

- They can never seem to **enjoy** what they have – since they are always obsessed over what they don't have.

- They walk around with a **chip** on their shoulders – because they feel that they are victims.

- They keep thinking that the world **owes** them something – so they assume that they have a right to things that don't belong to them and invariably turn to crime or similar vices.

In England (like most countries in the West) we live in one of the richest countries in the world, and our children are amongst the richest kids on the planet. Let your children know that. Teach them to appreciate the wealth they have.

- Eating 3 square meals a day is wealth

- Having running water from the tap is wealth

- Having a personal computer at home is wealth

- Being dropped at school in a car or bus is wealth

- Going to school to learn 5 days a week is wealth

- Having 4 or 5 pairs of shoes under their bed is wealth

- Light that comes on when you flip a switch is wealth

- Having battery-operated toys to play with is wealth.

Show them pictures of how children from the other side of the world live – or better still, take them there for their summer holidays. You may be surprised to see what the contrast will do for their impressionable souls.

If you do these things faithfully and consistently (and with God's help), you would be instilling a deep sense of appreciation into your children's psyche, and they will leave home with a sense of gratitude in their toolbox of life.

"Gratitude is not only the greatest of virtues, but the parent of all others." — Marcus Tullius Cicero

CHAPTER 4

Our Children Need A Sense Of Identity

Anyone who belongs to Christ becomes a new person. The old life is gone; a new life has begun...
(2 Corinthians 5:17.)

Our children come into the world with a personality, but not with an identity. Their personality will often get more distinct with age, but their identity will be formed by the people, places and things they are exposed to.

That's the reason God, in His boundless wisdom, arranged that parents would get the first opportunity to mould the identity of their children.

Identity is about answering the question, "Who am I?" or "How do I see myself?". It is the mental image we have of ourselves. It defines how we view ourselves or how we choose to identify ourselves – socially, economically, educationally or culturally.

The way our children see themselves will determine and mould their identity too. But the way they see themselves often comes from the way others close to them see them. That's means that your children are most likely to derive their identity from how you (the parent) treat or deal with them.

An impressive array of psychologists now agree that the core of our children's identity and self-esteem come from what we say to them in their formative years – whether positive or negative.

If that is true, and I believe it is, the question we should be asking ourselves is "What are we saying to our children?" Do they only hear our voice when we are upset with them or do we balance the need to tell them off with generous doses of healthy praises and affirmations?

If the only time your children hear you speaking to them is when you are reprimanding them or telling them off, chances are that their sense of identity will be skewed by the feeling that they are not good enough.

They will start to believe that they are not brilliant, not gifted, not desirable, not lovable, and not as good as someone else who they are being compared with.

Your children's sense of identity is so important because it will affect their self-esteem too. If children see themselves as loved, valued and accepted by those they look up to, 9 out of 10 times they will have a good sense of who they are. And, their self-esteem will remain healthy.

If our children know that it is okay to be themselves; to dream big; to be different or to have their own opinions, they will develop the courage to thrive. If they know that they are loved unconditionally, it would reflect in how they treat (or love) themselves. It will also impact on how they treat others around them.

In short, Children with a healthy self-esteem tend to:

- Be more creative, innovative and productive.

- Respond to situations in their life more positively.

- Display a more pragmatic and balanced attitude to life.

- Avoid the temptation to medicate on alcohol and drugs.

- Feel good about themselves and look after themselves.

- See themselves in a positive light and project their positive feelings onto others—resulting in healthier and better relationships.

As parents, we can go one better: We can help our children gain an identity and esteem that is anchored on the love of God for them. We can teach that God loves them unconditionally and help them value themselves based on that truth. Children that catch it, exercise a level of courage that is out of this world. I know this is what you want for your children or else you would not be reading this book.

We can strengthen our children's sense of identity by:

- **Affirming them**: Children desperately need to know that they valuable, beautiful, precious, loved, wanted, fearfully and wonderfully made, etc. They get it from our words; from our affirmations; from our praises; and from our loving and approving smiles.

- **Empowering them**: We can do that by entrusting them with more and bigger responsibilities. For instance, let them have their own pocket money as early as possible. Let them pick up some shopping for you as soon as they can go out on their own. Give them their own house keys as soon as prudently possible. Little and large responsibilities empower them to shine – which is what every parent wants.

- **Appreciating them**: Appreciating your children, shows them that you care; that you are aware of their effort; and that their attitude or behaviour is recognised. When your children act or behave in loving, compassionate, kind or sacrificial ways, we need to show them that we appreciate their good behaviour. When good behaviour gets rewarded, children are encouraged to keep behaving in similar ways.

- **Acknowledging them**: One of the main reasons incarcerated young offenders give for getting into gangs or into trouble is their desire to get affirmed, acknowledged or recognised. Children who are ignored at home look for attention and value elsewhere. Those who are acknowledge feel valued and are less likely to stray.

- **Passing down the family heritage**: The first thing that forms a child's sense of identity is his family. So if your child is proud of his family, his identity is more likely to stay intact. If you can find things in your family linage that can make your child feel special (like acts of bravery, achievements, heroism, fame, or spirituality), share it with him/her. Let your child know that he/she has 'pedigree' and linage to be grateful for.

You can help your children develop a strong sense of identity in a variety of other ways too.

For instance:

- You can paint a glorious picture of what they can become in life.

- You can teach them why they are unique and special to you and to God.

- You can praise them whenever they try something new or difficult.

- You can tell them uplifting stories from the family home, town or culture.

- You can find creative ways to show them how much you love them.

- You can even create a Family Lune with animals or symbols that represent the values, virtues and achievements of your family or yourself.

As my children were growing up, I personally did not find these last suggestions easy to do, because I didn't think I had much to boast about to my children. However, I did let them know that they were special to God and to me.

Once a young person has a sense of identity and belonging, I reckon that 80% of any potential problems are taken care of. Children who have a strong sense of identity are not easily swayed or led astray by fads, peer pressure or gang culture.

Instead, they are more likely to:

- Be bold and act courageously in life.

- Be more confident and self-assured.

- Be fearless, audacious and assertive.

- Get on and relate well with people.

- Be leaders amongst their peers; and

- Express their individuality, creativity and optimism more readily.

It's never too late to start building your children's self-esteem and sense of identity. So don't let your children leave home without a healthy sense of identity in their life's toolbox.

In the social jungle of human existence, there is no feeling of being alive without a sense of identity
– Erik Erikson

With a sense of identity comes purpose, and with purpose comes a focused and productive life
– Tony Peters

CHAPTER 5

Our Children Need A Sense of Humour

Rejoice in the Lord always. Again I will say, rejoice! (Philippians 4:4.)

Someone once defined humour as the ability to see the funny side of life. When we have a sense of humour, we can laugh at ourselves without developing a chip on our shoulders. We can see the funny side of life and maintain a smile even when things are tough.

Humour helps us to decompress. It relieves stress and it takes our minds off the pressures and seriousness of life. That's why our children need to have a good sense of humour in their life's toolbox.

Your children are going to experience the full range of what life is all about. They will experience joy and frustration; love and pain; excitement and fear; courage and discouragement; kindness and wickedness, new births and premature deaths. No one can avoid these opposing emotions, because they are all part of our life existence.

A good sense of humour therefore, is a great asset to have as your children navigates through the ups and downs and highs and lows of life. The Bible even likens the effect of humour to medicine.

Solomon put it this way: ***A merry heart does good, like medicine, but a broken spirit dries the bones.*** (Proverbs 17:22.)

The New Living Translation says it more clearly. It says, ***"A cheerful heart is good medicine, but a broken spirit saps a person's strength."*** That means that humour not only aids the healing process, but it can restore our strength when we are exhausted or depleted.

Humour also produces joy. And, joy produces strength, endurance and tenacity. The prophet of old put it this way: ***The joy of the Lord is your strength...*** (Nehemiah 8:10.)

The ability to laugh, see the funny side of life and laugh at one's self:

- Reduces the likelihood of heart disease.

- Boosts and strengthens the immune system.

- Improves mood swings and increases joy.

- Releases feel-good endorphins into our system.

- Increases the body's ability to produce antibodies.

- Relieves pain, lowers depression and relaxes the body.

- Neutralises tension and lowers stress (including blood pressure.)

- Improves breathing and burns calories (equals a mini-workout).

- Can improve a person's social life – as it makes them more likeable.

How can we help our children develop a sense of humour?

We can help our children develop a sense of humour by intentionally doing several things:

- **Learn to smile and laugh a lot yourself**

  Make sure that you don't allow the pressures and challenges of life to paint a permanent frown on your face. Don't make a habit of camping on the serious aspects of life alone. Look out for the funny side of life. Let it touch you. Let it make you laugh. Share your insights, joys and jokes with your children and laugh heartily with them.

- **Watch humorous programmes, movies or videos with your children**

  Not everyone takes to humour naturally. But everyone can learn to laugh at the right things. For some it might be a Tom & Jerry cartoon. For others it might be old re-runs of the 'Bill Cosby Show', 'Some Mothers Do 'Ave' Em, 'The Middle', 'Mr Bean' or 'Everybody Hates Chris'. Find what turns your children on and indulge with them in it. It's not uncommon for these programmes to give rise to great teaching moments too.

- **Do a lot of fun things together**

  If you can afford it, take them to theme parks like Disney World, Universal Studios, Alton Towers, Chessington World of Adventure or Pleasure Island. Even if you can't afford these places, take them to the local park, zoo, farm, museum, theatre, or athletics competitions. When you return home, have a chat and a laugh about what happened or what they observed.

Set time aside to look through old photographs or school projects, Year Books or Magazines, or anything that creates fun memories. Talk about things that fascinate them. Tickle them, if they are refusing to cooperate and if it is appropriate. (For instance, it may not be appropriate for a dad to be tickling his 16 year-old daughter.)

If you want your children to develop and maintain a sense of humour, they must know that it is okay to laugh and giggle in the home. That wouldn't happen if you can't stand a little noise from your children. So you must be willing to appreciate the value of a little joyful noise around the house, and not shut it down like we parents often do.

The best way to show children that giggling, laughing and enjoying humour is okay is to do it with them. Ideally, you want your children to enjoy several belly laughs every day.

The good news is that you are already a good parent. You want what is best for your child or children. Don't feel guilty if you didn't know what to do in the past. Now you do, so just make a start.

It's never too late to laugh with our children. And, if you succeed in helping them to develop a great sense of humour, you would be rewarded with children who can light up the dark with their presence and stay on top of life's anxieties and stresses.

So don't let your children leave home without a contagious sense
of humour.

**The only way to survive the hash realities of life on
earth is to develop a positive sense of humour.**

CHAPTER 6

Our Children Need A Sense Of Adventure

Don't be anxious about anything...
(Philippians 4:6.)

Anxiety does not empty tomorrow of its sorrows, but only empties today of its strength
– Charles Spurgeon

Children are naturally inquisitive and adventurous until we, their parents, mindlessly smother the fire of adventure out of them by crying wolf. Children want to explore and conquer their environment. I believe God made them that way, so they can discover and learn enough to make them victors in life from an early age.

When your child wants to know what is on top of the cabinet – he starts to climb up the side of it. When he is curious to see who is at the door – he tries to unlock it. Children will attempt to scale anything that looks interesting. They will even climb up the side of a skyscraper if you let them.

Why? Because they are fearless! Children are intrepid and audacious. They don't know fear or failure until adults introduce it to them; or tell them that they can't do something that they believe they can do.

For instance, your child starts to climb on a chair to scrutinise the television. What do you do? If you are like I was, you raise your voice by 50 decibels and shout out his name. Toby! Toby!! DON'T!!! DON'T!!!! Do you want to kill yourself? Get down! NOW!! I said, GET DOWN NOW!!!

The words we speak to our children during those formative years can build their confidence or destroy it. Studies show that for every positive sentence toddlers hear from their parents, they hear up to 10 negatively charged ones.

Words and phrases like:

- NO! NO!! NO!!!
- DON'T! DON'T!!
- YOU MUSTN'T DO THAT...
- YOU SHOULDN'T DO THIS...
- STOP DOING THIS! STOP DOING THAT!!
- DO YOU WANT TO KILL YOURSELF?
- DON'T GIVE ME A HEART ATTACK!

Imagine what is happening in the soul of a child who continues to hear these words barked at him 20 or even 40 times a day, from the people he trusts the most? What do you think he will eventually do?

You're right: He will stop being inquisitive and adventurous. He will learn that adventure is bad because it annoys his Mum. Being inquisitive is wrong because it makes his Dad angry. And worst of all, that kind of behaviour always gets him into trouble.

That's how we snuff that God-given, inbred sense of adventure out of our children. Let them explore a little; they will not die. Even if they fall, they will be okay because their bones are pliable and designed to make them bounce back – when they are young.

If truth be told, we parents are mostly to blame for many of the phobias our children end up having.

Of course, I am not suggesting that you should allow your children to do anything they want. That would be highly irresponsible. I am saying, however, that you need to be careful not to overload your children with scores of 'NOS' and 'DON'TS' everyday. Be careful not to transfer your fears and phobias onto their sensitive souls.

Chose carefully the things you forbid. For every negative thing you say 'NO' to, find something positive that you can say 'YES' to. In other words, your children should not just know what they are not allowed to do, they should know all the positive and creative things they are allowed (and even encouraged) to do.

Ask yourself whether your children have a dozen things that they love doing. Are those things opening them up to adventure and discovery. Most kids only have toys that keep them occupied, instead of toys that would keep them learning and creating.

If you want your children to have a sense of adventure you must help them find things they like that can stimulate them to more discovery and more learning. Of course, you would need to take your children's temperament, character traits, skills, likes and dislikes, and tendencies into consideration.

For instance, when my son was about 7 years old, he came home one day and asked if we could buy him a musical instrument. Within a couple of months, he was showing an above average ear for music. That is when it dawned on me that his future was going to hinge around music.

You too may have to watch out for your children's gifts and skills to determine what you might be able to do to give them a head start in their area of interest.

If you sense that your daughter loves talking or shows interest in learning languages; it will make sense to get her her own personal Scrabble or Thesaurus or Word Game or Language Box.

If your son is strangely attracted to your expensive tools or shows interest in science; it makes sense to get him his own Science Kit or Tool Box or Art & Craft Set.

Don't allow your children to live a boring life. Don't plump them in front of the television all day long. Instead, give them a legacy of opportunities to explore, to learn, and to grow. Children that have opportunities like this stand a better chance of making huge positive contributions to society when they grow up.

The important thing is to maximise your investment in your children, by choosing games, artefacts, toys, and visits to interesting places, that would help them grow their curiosity and sense of adventure.

Once your child gets turned on to a life of adventure and discovery, there is no telling what he or she might become. But one thing is certain, dozens of doors will open to that child; and he or she will have options to excel and succeed in areas that may not be open to other children.

If you encourage your children to explore freely and not be scared into submission, they will develop a useful sense of adventure. And, who knows, they may even discover something new that puts your family name on the map forever.

Don't let your children leave home without a palpable sense of adventure.

Life is either a great adventure or nothing
– Helen Keller

CHAPTER 7

Our Children Need A Sense Of Family Pride

Children should not have to provide
for their parents, but parents should
provide for their children.
(2 Corinthians 12:14.) Good News

One last tool that I believe our children need before they leave home is a sense of family pride. Modern studies and surveys are constantly showing us that family pride is a key contributor to the wellbeing of a well-balanced and healthy child.

The opposite of a sense of family pride is a sense of family shame. Children who feel ashamed of their family, their culture or their heritage are prone to erratic behaviour for most of their lives.

Typically, they hide their identity, change or shorten their name, don't invite their friends to their home, and don't talk about their family. Worst still, they become aloof or lie about who they really are.

On the other hand, children who exhibit family pride fair much better in these important areas of healthy personality development. Researchers are discovering again and again that children (especially teenagers) who are proud of their core family and who see their family life as great or very good:

- Are much happier and settled in school
- Are less aggressive and disruptive
- Have higher attendance averages
- Have better overall grades
- Are less likely to play truant
- Miss less days of school because of sickness
- Are less likely to join a troublesome gang
- Are less likely to get suspended from school
- Are less likely to get addicted to drugs or alcohol
- Are more likely to go all the way to Higher Education or University.

The sense of pride I am talking about is not the kind that looks down its nose on everyone else. I am not talking about arrogance, snobbery, conceit, disdain for authority, or an attitude of self-importance.

When I talk about a sense of family pride, I am talking about the positive satisfaction that people have in their family, heritage or upbringing—that leads to dignity, self-respect and good behaviour.

When I was growing up, our parents would sit many of us down on our first day back to school, and remind us that we were going out there to represent the family.

"Remember who's son (or daughter) you are." – our parents would say.

"Whatever you do out there will reflect on the family, so behave yourself."

"Don't put us to shame!" *"Remember that our family name is respected all over this town."*

That pet talk always helped us to think about the family reputation or the family name. It certainly made me think twice each time I wanted to misbehave as a youngster. I personally think it is a pity that many more parents these day don't do much to maintain or magnify the family institution.

Every child (and adult for that matter) needs to feel that they belong to something bigger than themselves. And, family can be the first 'bigger' thing they grow up belonging to. Make sure your children are proud of their family. Make sure you make them proud by the way you carry yourself; the way you talk; the way you dress; and the way your behave in front of them.

I remember being very ashamed of my family when I was young because I knew that the neighbours often heard my parents arguing and quarrelling. I was ashamed because my father often spoke at the top of his voice and disturbed the neighbours whenever he came home upset or drunk.

I was ashamed because the landlord had to come knocking at our door at odd hours and multiple times, if he ever wanted to collect his rent. I was ashamed because everyone who knew us knew that my dad was probably having an affair with the women they saw in his vehicle.

Nevertheless, I am so grateful to God that the shame only made me more determined not to repeat the mistakes I observed in my family.

The family doesn't need to be rich or popular or in politics to be a child's source of pride and joy. It's what you show and tell your child or children that will create the image they carry. It's how you carry yourself and how you live your life in front of them.

Single Parent homes

I know that more and more homes are single parent families. My heart goes out to mums and dads who find themselves in this rather challenging position of raising children on their own. God designed the family to work better with a mum and a dad – living and loving their children together. That is still the ideal family structure according to God's plan.

However, children from single parent families can still have massive family pride, because it's twice as difficult for one parent to carry the burden of child rearing. So, if for example, a single parent mother is committed to a dignified and respectable life before her children, their sense of pride in their mother's effort and sacrifices could be huge.

Although it may be harder for single parents to juggle all the responsibilities of raising children, they can still do a really great job if their priorities are really well defined. Married people may have a slight advantage when it comes to raising children only if the marriage is healthy and mature. But half of all marriages are not healthy or mature.

Married people have many more responsibilities and distractions to fit around their lives. When you are married you have to create time for your spouse, your in-laws, your spouse's friends, Anniversaries, family holidays, and the like. If you are a single parent, you probably don't have all of that. So you can invest a lot of that saved time and energy into your children.

The point I am making is that, if you are a single parent you don't have to feel that you have a huge disadvantage. Yes, there may be some areas you wish you had the help of a companion, but you can make it up for your children in other ways.

I know of several single parents whose children have turned out exceptionally well. And, I know of several married couples whose children have fallen off the grid – so to speak. What made the crucial difference, is what each child left home with or without.

Our children are very resilient. They can bounce back from unimaginable tragedy, disappointment and pain. But all the resilience in the world wouldn't take a child over the finished line in one piece without the seven tools we have discussed in this book.

IN CONCLUSION

Our children need tool to help them excel in their relationships, in decision-making, in their finances, in their roles in society and in their responsibilities as parents to the next generation. They need the tools to help them stay faithful and committed to God, to find and collaborate successfully with a spouse, to excel in the market place, to live a balanced and healthy life, to help them develop a life of integrity, and manage their future home.

For all these virtues, they need:

- A Solid Foundation For Faith
- A Sense Of Purpose
- A Sense Of Gratitude
- A Sense Of Identity
- A Sense of Humour
- A Sense Of Adventure, and

- A Sense Of Family Pride

So, don't let your children leave home without these character-enhancing and life-lifting tools. Remember, it's never too late to start the process.

But you are not like that, for you are a chosen people. You are royal priests, a holy nation, God's very own possession. As a result, you can show others the goodness of God, for he called you out of the darkness into his wonderful light. "Once you had no identity as a people; now you are God's people. Once you received no mercy; now you have received God's mercy."
(1 Peter 2:9-10.) NLT

Helpful Exercises To Get You Started

1.) List 5 important thoughts you are taking away from this book?

____

____

____

____

____

2.) What can you put in place with your child (or children) to help them develop a sense of faith on the reality of God?

____

____

____

3.) How can you help your children develop a sense of purpose?

____

____

____

4.) What practical examples can you use to help your child become very grateful for what he or she has?

____

____

____

5.) Write down 4/5 statements you can say to your child every morning or evening that can strengthen his or her sense of identity.

____

____

____

____

____

6.) How can you make sure that a healthy sense of humour is valued and exercised in your home regularly?

____

____

____

____

____

7.) Plan an 'Adventure' party or outing for your child at least once a month. Make it something that your child looks forward to. (e.g. It could be something as simple as going to try a different flavour of ice cream next month.)

____

____

____

____

____

8.) Speak to older members of your family. Ask them about any great events, achievements, or famous people from the

family. Write what you learn down and gradually share
them with your child as the opportunity presents itself.

____

____

____

____

____

From the Author

Thank you again for purchasing this book.
If you enjoyed reading it (and I certainly hope you did),
I would appreciate it if you would rate it fairly for me
and for the benefit of other potential readers—and
post a short review on any of the sites that sell it.

www.rocksolidmarriages.com

Thank you very much!

Other Books by the Author

Secrets of a Lasting Marriage – 7 Vital Building Blocks for a Healthy Marriage

How to Build a Rock Solid Marriage – Choices That Will Give You the Marriage of Your Dreams

Ten Keys to Effective Communication in Marriage

Stress No More – 20 Healthy Ways To Reduce Stress, Anxiety & Worry

Maximising Your Season of Singleness – Using Your Season of Singleness to Prepare for Marriage

Keeping God At The Centre Of Your Marriage – Simple Ways To Keep God At The Centre Of Your Relationship

How to Rescue Your Marriage from Breaking Up – Avoiding the Ten Major Relationship Killers

Find Your Soul Mate God's Way – Say Goodbye To Dating

21 Crucial Things They Don't Teach Young People About Sex

Seven Tools Your Children Should Not Leave Home Without – Equipping Your Children to Excel

Understand Your Marriage Vows - What the Marriage Vows Mean and How to Honour Them

Why God Wants You & Your Family in a Life-giving Church – 12 Reasons to Get Involved in a Great Local Church…

Why Can't We Talk About It? – 4 Practical Steps to Help Reduce Misunderstandings During Conversations by Shola Peters

How to Find a Life-giving Church – You Can Thrive in

All books are available at
good Bookshops and Audiobook Platforms